Farm Animals

★ A very first picture book ★

For a free color catalog describing Gareth Stevens Publishing's list of high-quality books and multimedia programs, call 1-800-542-2595 (USA) or 1-800-461-9120 (Canada). Gareth Stevens Publishing's Fax: (414) 225-0377.

Library of Congress Cataloging-in-Publication Data

Farm animals: a very first picture book / consultant, Nicola Tuxworth.
    p. cm. — (Pictures and words)
  Includes bibliographical references and index.
  Summary: Simple text and photographs present farm animals and their young, including cows, horses, and goats.
  ISBN 0-8368-2271-4 (lib. bdg.)
  1. Domestic animals—Juvenile literature. [1. Domestic animals. 2. Animals—Infancy.] I. Title. II. Series.
  SF75.5.F38   1999
  636—dc21   98-31773

This North American edition first published in 1999 by
Gareth Stevens Publishing
1555 North RiverCenter Drive, Suite 201
Milwaukee, WI 53212 USA

Original edition © 1996 by Anness Publishing Limited. First published in 1996 by Lorenz Books, an imprint of Anness Publishing Inc., New York, New York. This U.S. edition © 1999 by Gareth Stevens, Inc. Additional end matter © 1999 by Gareth Stevens, Inc.

Senior editor/text: Caroline Beattie
Special photography: Lucy Tizard
Design and typesetting: Michael Leaman

Picture credits: Bruce Coleman/Mark N. Boulton: sheepdog; Bruce Coleman/Hans Reinhard: cow and calf, goat and kids, cat; Trip/H. Rogers: duck and ducklings; Zefa Picture Library (UK) Ltd.: sow and piglets, ewe and lamb.

Printed in Mexico

1 2 3 4 5 6 7 8 9 03 02 01 00 99

Farm Animals

★ A very first picture book ★

Nicola Tuxworth

Gareth Stevens Publishing
MILWAUKEE

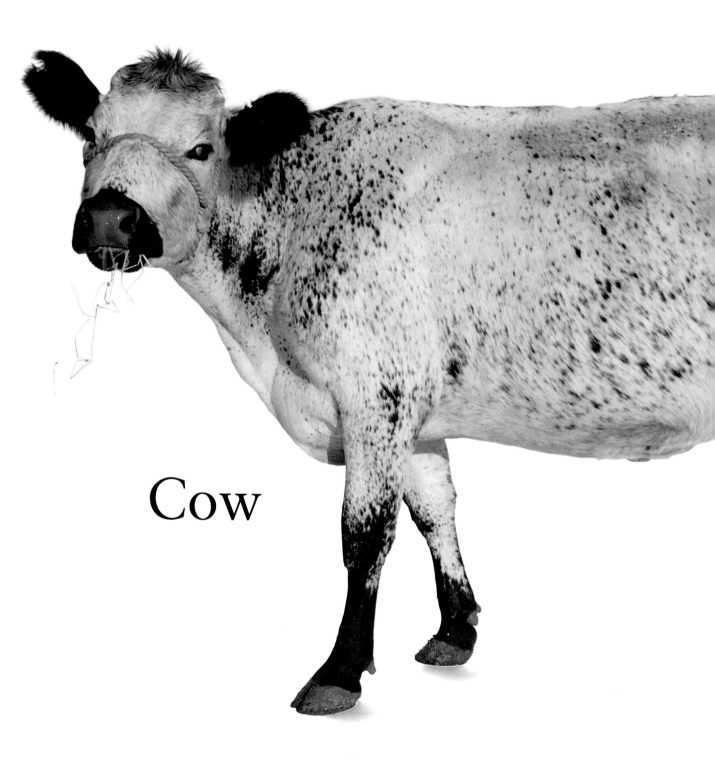

Cow

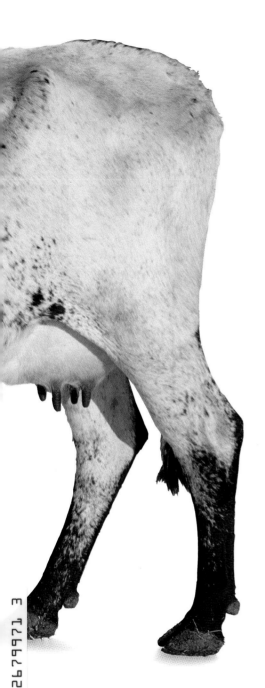

A baby cow is called a calf. Calves drink their mother's milk.

5

Horse

A baby horse is called
a foal. It eats grass just
like its mother.

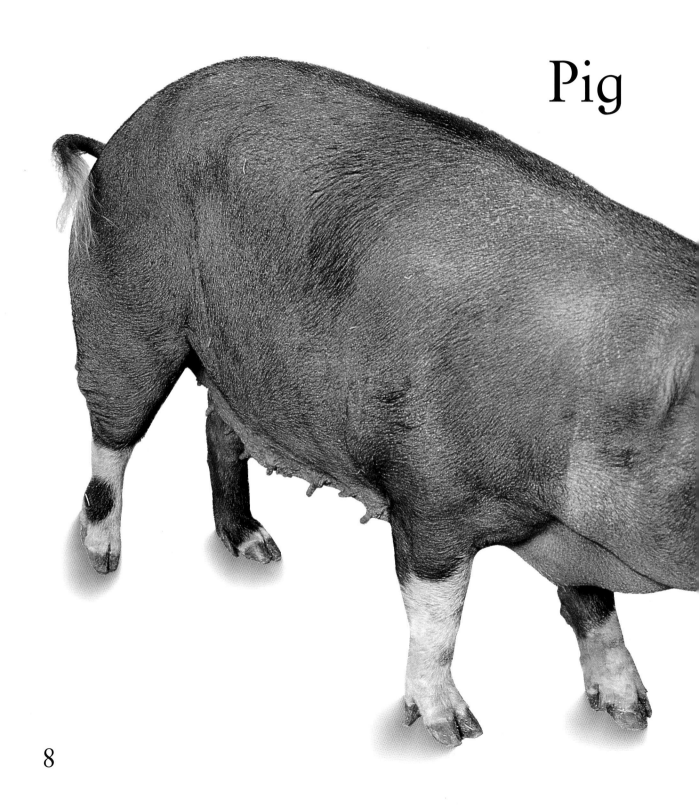

Pig

8

Mother pigs have little piglets. They root around in the ground to find things to eat.

Sheep

Little lambs nuzzle up close to
their mothers for comfort.
They feel warm and safe.

Goat

Mother goats
have twin babies
called kids.

Duck

Ducklings stay in the nest with their mother. They will soon take a swim.

Chicken

Chickens lay eggs.
Fluffy chicks hatch
out of them.

Dog

A dog helps the
shepherd bring
the sheep home.

Cat

Cats keep all the
mice away.

It's Saturday night —
time for a bath!

Questions for Discussion

1. Can you think of any animals, besides the ones shown in this book, that live on a farm?

2. What does each farm animal in this book eat?

3. Which of the farm animals in this book have two legs? Which of them have four legs? Which have wings?

4. Find the picture of the mother cow with her baby calf. Look at the pictures of the other farm animals in this book. What is the name for each of the other mother animals?

5. In what ways are baby ducklings different from their mother? In what ways are the ducklings and their mother the same?

More Books to Read

Animals Are Not Like Us (series). Graham Meadows (Gareth Stevens)

At the Farm. Look Once, Look Again (series). David M. Schwartz (Gareth Stevens)

Cows. Mary Ann McDonald (Child's World)

Farm Animals. Animals at a Glance (series). Isabella Dudek (Gareth Stevens)

My First Visit to a Farm. José Maria Parramón (Barron's)

Real Baby Animals (series). Gisela and Siegfried Buck (Gareth Stevens)

Videos

Babe. (MCA Universal Home Video)

Barnyard Babies. (Video-11)

Farm Animals. (Good Apple)

Farm Animals and Their Mothers. (Phoenix/BFA)

Web Sites

www.usda.gov/nass/nasskids /games/topstck/tpstck.htm

www.davisfarmland.com

Some web sites stay current longer than others. For further web sites, use your search engines to locate the following topics: *cats, chickens, cows, dogs, ducks, farm animals, goats, horses, pigs,* and *sheep.*

Glossary-Index

calf: the name for a baby born to certain animals, such as cows. (p. 5)

comfort: a feeling of being safe and taken care of. (p. 11)

duckling: a baby or young duck. (p. 15)

fluffy: having hair or feathers that are soft, light, and airy. (p. 17)

foal: a baby or young horse. (p. 7)

hatch: to come into life out of an egg. (p. 17)

kid: a baby goat. (p. 13)

lamb: a baby sheep. (p. 11)

nuzzle: to rub or touch something gently with the nose. (p. 11)

piglet: a baby pig. (p. 9)